How to Take Minutes *of* Meetings

How to Take Minutes *of* Meetings

Jennie Hawthorne

First published in 1993
Reprinted 1996

Kogan Page Limited
120 Pentonville Road
London N1 9JN

British Library Cataloguing in Publication Data

A CIP record for this book is available from the British Library.

ISBN 0-7494-1120-1

Typeset by BookEns Ltd, Baldock, Herts.
Printed and bound in Great Britain by Clays Ltd, St Ives plc.

Contents

Introduction

Minute taking is an important but under-rated part of business management. The person responsible for taking the minutes records the place, date and time of a particular meeting, the names of the persons attending, any decisions made, and how, when and by whom they are to be carried out. The minutes are therefore like a historical document. The more important the meeting, the more important it is to make an accurate transcript of what was said, and by whom.

Cabinet meetings are on a different level of importance from a meeting of sports-club members but, in both cases, the people present and others who have an interest in the event want a record of it.

In view of the need for accuracy, you may wonder why a tape-recorder is not used for taking minutes, or why everything said at a meeting should not be taken down in shorthand. Important meetings do have shorthand notes or a tape-recorder as a back-up to the written minutes, but a full shorthand transcript could take up as many pages as the novelist Proust needed to describe a person turning over in bed . . . and prove nothing like as readable. A transcript taken down in shorthand and then typed (or printed) verbatim, before summarising, is not the most efficient or economic way of communicating to a large number of participants what went on at a meeting they attended. And for those who think a tape-recording alone is sufficient, the following tale may illustrate why this device will never entirely displace the human minute taker, and might even lead to a management crisis.

A big firm was in the habit of having a monthly 'consultative committee' meeting. Some 40 members from various sections of the company used to attend. As is the usual practice, the minutes were written up after the meeting. And as is, alas, quite often the case, the minutes took so long to distribute that they arrived seconds before the new meeting was due to begin, and sometimes even later than that.

Everybody got impatient with this delay and a new system was requested. It was agreed therefore that the next meeting should be taped. The proceedings would be written up as soon as possible after the meeting, exactly as they came out on tape. This was done. The typewritten minutes were transcribed word for word from the tape-recording. They reached the committee members only a couple of days after the meeting took place. Were the members satisfied? They were most definitely not. Pandemonium erupted. Fierce denials broke out about what was said and by whom. There were equally fierce protests about who was to do what and when. The tape was therefore played back. It proved that the minute taker had faithfully written down every single word that was said. After listening to the tape, the members decided unanimously to go back to the old system whereby the minute taker gave not a blow-by-blow mention of every utterance but a fair summary of the proceedings. The minutes would be sent out as soon as possible before the next meeting. And so it was done.

This true story illustrates the importance attached to the minutes by those present at a particular meeting. But what if you are asked to take over this role for the first time, as in the example that follows? This deals with a new employee, but the situation is the same for anyone who has to take minutes for the first time.

You have just landed your first job. After three weeks you are still congratulating yourself for having got such a good post in the teeth of fierce competition, and for having survived in the office for a whole three weeks without making a major mishap. Your pay is due shortly, the first decent pay packet you've had since leaving college. Suddenly in comes the manager.

'You won't mind taking the minutes for the next marketing meeting, will you, Miss Craig?' he asks, if he is the polite type . . . or barking some similar order if he is not.

'Miss Sullivan, who usually does them for us,' he continues, 'is on sick leave.' He must have noticed your look of apprehension which you thought you had disguised, for he adds, 'It's only a matter of simple note taking. I'm sure you'll do it brilliantly.' You nod your head to show enthusiasm for this new task though inside you are in a panic. The boss moves out quickly before you have a chance to say a word.

Minutes? You've never taken a minute in your life, though you vaguely remember occasional committee meetings in college where there appeared to be somebody who took notes. You never heeded the note taker, because you were too interested in the people constantly interrupting the proceedings with the phrase, 'On a point of order, Mr Chairman'.

You now look in vain for a book, a leaflet, a brochure giving some information on the subject of minute taking. Does anybody in the office know about minute taking? As a newcomer on the staff, you want to appear knowledgeable, especially as you're not. When you do pick up courage to enquire where the minutes are kept, nobody seems to know.

You'll probably be able to find the old minutes before the next meeting but meanwhile, you feel as if you're floundering in a sea of ignorance. If the minutes are a record of what happens at a meeting, as you vaguely imagine they must be, should everything that is done or said be reported? If not, what does go in and what, if anything, should be left out?

Questions such as these are asked not only by Miss Craig in the above example. They are asked by everybody who, for the first time, has to take minutes at a meeting. The following chapters attempt to answer these questions and the others which arise in connection with the important task of compiling minutes.

CHAPTER 1
The Minutes: An Overview

This chapter gives an overview of minute taking by answering a few important questions.

What?

What are the minutes? Minutes are a summary of the following facts:

- The time and date of a meeting, where it was held, and the name of the person who chaired it.
- The names of all persons present, and apologies for absence from those who were asked or expected to attend the meeting but did not do so.
- All items discussed whether on the agenda or not.
- Any actions agreed upon, and who agreed to undertake them.
- The name of persons who assigned tasks to others, the name of those to whom the tasks were assigned, and the date of completion for the tasks, if known.

Documents of impromptu meetings are usually referred to as *records of meetings*. Though these meetings do not always rely on an agenda they do try to follow the conventions and principles used in taking minutes.

Visit reports are similar to the minutes of an ordinary meeting except that they record a visit where people meet to investigate certain points (such as the safety of a particular site for aircraft landings) and set out the findings that result from that visit.

Why?

Minutes are taken to provide a record for future use of discussions, events and decisions which happened at a meeting. They remind participants of what went on at a meeting they attended, and tell those who did not attend what happened. The minutes also provide a forum for continuous discussion of topics, which, without a written record, might otherwise be repeated at another meeting, forgotten or imperfectly remembered. They are also available for use as evidence in legal proceedings.

When?

Minutes usually are taken in note form during a meeting, then later typed or printed in more formal style and distributed to members. The minutes are validated and signed as a true and accurate record of the proceedings by the person who chaired the meeting, which might take place on a regular basis, such as monthly, or annually, as with public companies.

How?

Initially, the minutes may be taken down in shorthand, or taped by recorder. In the latter case there is always the risk that the tape might be damaged or lost. In the former, subsequent readers of the minutes might not be able to transcribe shorthand into normal text. So whether the minutes are first taken down in shorthand or longhand or taped, they are eventually always typed (or for a large organisation, printed). They are then stored in the appropriate place and copies made for later distribution. More information on how the minutes should be written is given in later chapters.

Where?

The minutes are recorded wherever a meeting takes place. This place may be chosen by the person who chairs the meeting but who often delegates the task to a secretary or other person who appears suitable. The place chosen for a meeting can be in a room within the office or factory or outside in a conference hall, hotel or similar venue depending on the numbers and personnel who are expected to attend.

Who?

The person who takes the minutes can be anybody who is asked, who volunteers or to whom this role is given by the person convening or chairing the meeting. It may be somebody within an office, who is known to take shorthand, and for this reason appears to be a desirable person for the task. Taking the minutes may be part of a person's specific duties, or it may be somebody brought in for a specific occasion.

Who attends the meetings at which minutes are recorded depends on the type of meeting. For general meetings of a limited company, it will be the directors and shareholders.

CHAPTER 2
Functions of the Minutes

Minutes are expected to provide an accurate summary of what went on at a meeting, to transmit information to people unable to attend it, inform members of the next meeting and provide a record of decisions taken, and how those decisions were reached. These functions can be summarised as constitutional, executive and continuous.

Constitutional

The minutes, when signed, provide an authentic record of the proceedings. This is the constitutional function of the minutes.

Executive

When something has been decided, that decision will have to be carried out, and probably within a given timespan. The minute taker must note down the name of the person to whom the task is assigned, who gave the assignment, and what date if any is envisaged for its completion . . . or perhaps a progress report. The minutes therefore constitute a record of any action to be taken and the authority for doing it. This is the executive function of the minutes.

Continuous

Policy is discussed and progresses through a meeting or a succession of meetings. The minutes should therefore enable the final points of a policy discussion at the last meeting to be continued at the next, without any interruption save the time lag between the respective meetings. In this way, minutes act as a continuous or ongoing function for action.

Arising out of the above functions it can be seen that minutes must provide an accurate, brief account of the proceedings. They need to be written in clear and precise prose, and in an orderly fashion for easy reading.

Contents of the minutes

What should go into the minutes is partly governed by the rules of the organisation and the order of business to be dealt with at the meeting. This order of business is known as the *agenda,* or items to be followed. It may be compiled by the Chair or by the Chair with the help of the secretary or minute taker. If you are taking the minutes you are expected to be able to refer to the rules or at least have a copy of them when you attend a meeting.

Some meetings such as those of parliamentary debates recorded in *Hansard* give a word-for-word account of the proceedings. Other minutes such as those at company board meetings provide the briefest summary consistent with legal requirements. As a minute taker you will probably have to adopt a line midway between these two extremes, giving an accurate précis of the proceedings and dispensing with all the verbiage often wrapped round the actual point under discussion.

Very useful guidelines on what goes into minutes is contained in the following extract on the subject from the Director General of the Health and Safety Executive:

- When writing minutes, do not attribute statements to particular people or groups unless this is essential either because no one else agreed or because a particular authority belongs to the originator. Say 'In further discussion, the following points were made, (a), (b), (c) etc.'

- *Never* include verbiage such as 'Opening the meeting, the chairman said,' or 'Welcoming Mr X . . . etc.' What does it add?
- Use your discretion. Never put nonsense into someone's mouth even if he did talk nonsense. In the extreme case, omit the point. In a less extreme case, expand that part of what was said that did make sense. Minutes are properly NOT a record of what took place, but of how agreement was reached or disagreement arose; usually agreement is founded on the sense that was talked.

Requirements of the minutes

Minutes need to be accurate, brief and clear. They also need to be objective, showing no political or other bias.

Accuracy

Unless the meeting is a strictly formal one where every word is being transcribed, you will need to understand what is going on in order to summarise the proceedings accurately. This is especially true for policy decisions which get such a wide degree of support that there is no need for a vote. A good rule in such situations is when there is no need for a vote, take a note. In other words, the minute taker should register this consensus and how it came about, and not ignore the decision or what led up to it because no vote was taken. If memory is relied upon, and no record made of such a consensus and how it came about, recriminations could arise later. To avoid this unhappy scenario, ask for clarification of any point not clear to you, or about any aspect of a decision which you do not understand, and record it immediately. Note down the names of all the main speakers, in initials if need be.

Balance

How frank should the minutes be? Even when they are confidential or 'top secret' they should still provide an accurate record of what took place at a meeting. To do this and at the same time give the flavour or tone of the event is no easy feat, particularly if arguments get heated and the sentiments expressed, become abusive. People holding strong political views are very partisan, as are the innovators of a particular idea or project.

Though the minutes may not necessarily record the actual words spoken, the tone of the meeting needs to be expressed, along with the arguments, if any, that took place. In such cases, unless someone is physically ejected or the meeting ends in disarray, it is often wiser not to mention people by name but, if they are mentioned, make particularly sure that right names are minuted. When a meeting is confidential, or parts of it are information sensitive, the minutes are sent out to certain members only and headed either 'secret' or 'confidential'. Sometimes such confidential information has a note, such as 'for distribution only after . . .' followed by a date. Or it may be recorded on coloured paper to differentiate it from the rest of the minutes.

Brevity

Are you good at précis? A précis is a summary in the précis writer's own words. Both précis writing and writing the minutes have to convey facts or ideas to others as briefly and accurately as possible.

Can you distinguish between what is important and what is not? These are the hallmarks of an excellent minute taker. It is no good being so brief, however, that little of intelligence is conveyed to the reader so that he or she has no idea of what went on. If your minutes show, for example, that a letter from the President of the Shove Halfpenny Club was read and discussed, is anybody any the wiser? What was the letter about? An offer or refusal of help, congratulations or blame? Summarise the points mentioned so that a later reader knows roughly the contents of the correspondence.

Clarity

If you abbreviate your notes in any way, make sure you know, and any later reader will know, what the abbreviations mean.

Places are more easily remembered than dates or times, so emphasise *the place* where an important decision was taken, for example:

- Minutes of a meeting held in Brussels (or the board room) on . . . .

When a meeting is held regularly in the same room, it is still necessary to mention that fact.

You may need to include recommendations not adopted, and the reasons for their rejection, particularly if the discussion arose around the contents of a background paper. In such a case, later readers may not be able to understand the discussion without this extra knowledge, so either outline the contents of the paper, attach it to the minutes or note its title for later reference.

Vocabulary

In writing the minutes you are hardly likely to produce a literary masterpiece, a gem that will inspire, entertain, amuse or even move the reader. Minutes are strictly functional. Their aim is to give an accurate, factual, succinct report of a meeting which took place, and which you are recording if not exactly for posterity (though that may be the case) but for interested readers. In whatever form the minutes are ultimately produced, they should be concise, correct, legible and intelligible.

Tense

Minutes are usually taken down in the past tense as, for example, 'decided', 'moved', 'explained'. This use of the past tense helps link a speaker to any comments he or she makes on a subject, thus:

Mr Jones said that he told the MP that much disquiet was felt over the plan to go ahead with the new road.

The imperfect tense as in 'was agreed', 'were expressed', when used in the minutes often gives a more objective and impartial flavour to the writing, which the context may require. The following is an example of this use of the imperfect tense:

> An interest was expressed in the idea of providing a Christmas hamper for retired members of the company.

Finally, 'would' can be used to denote an action that, agreed in committee, is to take place in the future. The following is an example:

> The ownership of the land would be as follows: Mrs G would retain the area 50 yards to the east of the present fence, BR would own the remainder.

CHAPTER 3
The Minute Taker

Questions

You can come to the role of minute taker by several paths. It might be part of your job, you may have volunteered for it or been asked to do it for a specific occasion, a local charity, sports club or other community association. No matter what has led you to take up this task, you will need to know, if you don't already, answers to the following questions:

- What is the object of the meeting?
- Who attends?
- How will it be conducted?
- Are there any special rules which you have to follow?
- Are you allowed to speak on any subject or is your role purely to record the discussions?
- Is there any order to be followed and who, if anyone, has control over what goes on?
- In essence, what are likely to be your duties?

Other questions which might trouble you if you are taking the minutes for the first time include the following:

- Whether you take and transcribe your own notes.
- When you are expected to have the first draft prepared.
- Whether an agenda has been sent out to all the relevant people (or indeed what an agenda is; see Chapter 4).
- Whether you have to send or phone the members to remind them of the date and time of the next meeting.
- Do you have to book a room, organise equipment and refreshments?

Previous minutes

If these can be found, they often provide answers to some at least of the above questions. They will certainly show you how the previous minutes were presented. Even if that presentation is not a model of its kind, some rules operated by the group will emerge. Previous minutes will also show you whether there is a special kind of jargon or vocabulary which the group uses, intelligible to them but well nigh incomprehensible to you as minute taker or to any other newcomer. A glossary is therefore provided on page 57 which gives, in alphabetical order, terms frequently used at formal meetings.

Duties of the minute taker

If answers to questions which trouble you cannot be found in any previous minutes, they may be discovered lurking in the rules of meetings as detailed in Chapter 5. Knowing or being able to refer to the rules will ease your way through the labyrinths of many company meetings. Your duties as a minute taker will, however, vary according to the position you hold within the company or the group. Some of the tasks you might be expected to perform include the following:

1. Recording attendance at meetings and providing the Chair with a list of the members present and any papers relating to the meeting.
2. Sorting out comments, suggested actions and decisions of the meeting, naming those delegated to carry them out.
3. Summarising the above.
4. Bringing the rules to the meeting for reference if needed.
5. Ensuring the safe keeping of the minutes and all related materials and that the records and documents associated with the meeting are signed by the Chair before he or she leaves.

You must therefore be able to do the following:

1. Write out an accurate summary of the decisions, comments and suggested actions (in line with point 2 above) which took place at the meeting. This must be completed within a reasonable period, and certainly before the next meeting.
2. Bring a copy of the rules to the meeting (as in point 4 above) and find previous mention of a topic if requested.
3. Record attendances and absences (as in point 1 above) and provide the Chair with a list of these names and any papers or correspondence relevant to the meeting.
4. Get all records and documents signed by the Chair as evidence of their authentication and store in safe keeping the minutes and any related material (as in point 5 above) except that assigned to others.

If the discussion is too fast for you to note it correctly, request the Chair to halt the meeting temporarily.

Qualities needed

It can be seen from the possible duties of a minute taker that he or she needs at least three major qualities and lots of minor ones. You should be a good listener, a critical thinker and an accurate, perceptive writer.

The duties of a minute taker appear so relatively simple, but that appearance is very deceptive, for minute taking is full of traps for the unwary.

Indeed, as well as having the three major qualities mentioned above, you need also to be alert, highly organised and able to concentrate on the discussions so that you can record accurately and objectively what takes place. Being able to understand company jargon is a skill worth acquiring, as is some knowledge of the topics under discussion. If you don't know the people attending the meeting you ought at least to know (or learn) the spelling and presentation of their names. In other words, you are expected to be a paragon of business virtue even if, in your opinion, your pay in no way reflects this eminence.

You may sometimes be allowed a voice in the proceedings, though this is not always the case. You can then contribute your ideas and opinions. This means it will be necessary for you to record as well as propose or discuss, unlike the majority of participants, who need merely listen or propose without having also to process what they have said. It is very difficult to participate *and* take notes, so enter into any discussion only when you feel it is vital to do so.

Problems of a minute taker

The following list comprises not the disadvantages (which are outweighed by the advantages) of being a minute taker so much as difficulties which arise within the meeting, and which in some cases are due to the participants. These difficulties include the following:

- Being asked to leave the meeting to do 'odd jobs' (take photocopies, phone for cabs, make coffee, etc).
- A Chair unable to keep order or keep the meeting within the time limit.
- Speakers who are disorganised: too fast, too indistinct or too verbose.
- More than one person speaking at a time.
- Distractions (noise of phones, traffic, aircraft).
- Chair or speaker not following the agenda.
- Too many items on the agenda.
- Speakers not identifying themselves or not being identified by the Chair.
- Negative, power hungry or unprepared people.
- Not being allowed a break when others get one.

Advantages of being a minute taker

In spite of the difficulties, which may never arise, when there is a good Chair the minute taker has certain special advantages. As a minute taker you have access to everyone in the group. This aspect of minute taking can provide you with very useful contacts, which can be particularly helpful in the future.

You learn what is going on in all parts of the organisation or group for which you are working. You can earn the thanks of the Chair and other committee members by helping them to achieve the aims of the meeting. Finally, through taking the minutes you can learn the art of précis writing and other communication skills which will be of use in future.

The minute-taker's image

Whatever your job, you need to project a successful image. First impressions count even if they are superseded by second impressions. Appearance and body language are especially important with business contacts. The following guidelines may help the new minute taker.

For the first meeting, dress conservatively. In your spare time you may be the best Rastafarian jazz player around, a footballer, rugby player or cricketer equal in brilliance to England's finest, but unless you are attending a fringe-arts or sports committee meeting, it is wiser not to let your attire spell out your enthusiasms. And even if you have won the model girl competition in Sodding on the Marsh, you don't need to emphasise your wonderful looks by wearing the latest bizarre fashions: your beauty will be obvious enough.

Make contact with members as they come in by greeting them when they arrive. Don't overdo the enthusiasm, for you will have to carry it through for everybody. When seated, don't hunch your shoulders or take up more than your fair share of space. Encourage those who are tentative or hesitant speakers, but whose opinions you wish to hear, by leaning forward and nodding. If you can't hear a certain speaker, cup your hand to your ear to indicate you want him or her to speak more loudly.

Cultivate, too, the art of the poker face so you don't show your emotions when you hear fatuous or foolish remarks. Don't inadvertently show by your lack of eye contact, a change in your facial expression or by body language your dislike of a particular speaker who might be ruled out of order in any event. Give everybody a cheerful but not too informal 'Good bye' when they leave.

Carry-in material

It looks more efficient (though it need not necessarily be so) if as a minute taker you bring in to the meeting a certain amount of material with you. This 'take-in material' can include extra copies of the agenda, for though you will have sent it out prior to the meeting there are always members who will have mislaid their copy. You should also have with you a list of the people who are coming (as noted above); a guide to the rules of the organisation; the minute book for the past year (if one exists); relevant correspondence and reports; a diary for noting important dates mentioned at the meeting; extra writing material and possibly coloured pens; a watch and (if allowed and you are happy with the machine) a tape-recorder and tapes.

Actions before the meeting

Before the meeting begins, the minute taker should attend to the following:

- Obtain or agree with the Chair the order of business, *date, time, place* of the meeting, and whether refreshments are necessary (for an illustration of double-column format, see page 32). Check the venue is available.
- Obtain copies of previous minutes, if available. Check venue against distribution list. (Is it large enough? Has the agenda given you by the Chair covered any points left undecided at last meeting?) If necessary, point out the need to alter the agenda.

- Check names on previous minutes. Consult with Chair over any deletions or additions (staff, addresses, titles etc).
- Send out forward notice of meeting, together with the suggested agenda, and the *time, date, day, place.* Emphasise latest date for any changes in agenda.
- Immediately prior to meeting, visit the venue and check whether there is sufficient seating, writing material, etc, available.

Booking the room

The booking or reservation of the room for a meeting can present a problem for a newcomer to the task. When there are no precendents or rules in previous minutes to guide you, take your courage in both hands and reserve a room as soon as the date of the next meeting is fixed. Check that the space and furnishings meet the requirements of the group:

- Is it the right size?
- Has it good lighting, with audio-visual equipment, if required?
- Is the venue appropriate for members, guests, speakers?

When you plan to use one of the company or organisation's rooms, book the room through the usual channels. Type a polite memo and stick it on the door the day before the meeting confirming that you will be using the room. This may bring repercussions, but better that than turning up at a room already occupied by possibly senior and eventually irate personnel.

Attendance

To save time at the start of the meeting, prepare an attendance list and make a plan of the seating arrangements. Give each person a number or initials beside their name. This makes for easier note taking. In large meetings, an attendance book is signed by each member on entry into the room. A common method of recording smaller attendances is to list the names under 'present and apologies for absence'. But what about absentees who do not apologise for absence? One way of getting round this difficulty is to list all members, distinguishing between those who sent apologies and those who sent none by a typographical device such as coloured ink, or a capital AR beside their names for apologies received . . . whatever sort of device tells you who was present, who absent and who sent apologies for absence.

Put full names of members present at the top of your minutes followed by bracketed initials so that, when the minutes are read, the attendees can be easily identified. If you are using numbers as a means of identifying who is present, tick off the participants' names as they appear and show them to their numbered seats. For less formal meetings, give them a number and let them find the appropriate place at the table themselves – but check that they are in the right place before the meeting begins. The minute taker should sit near the Chair so as to hear everything. The following is an example of table layout and the numbering (or initialling) system:

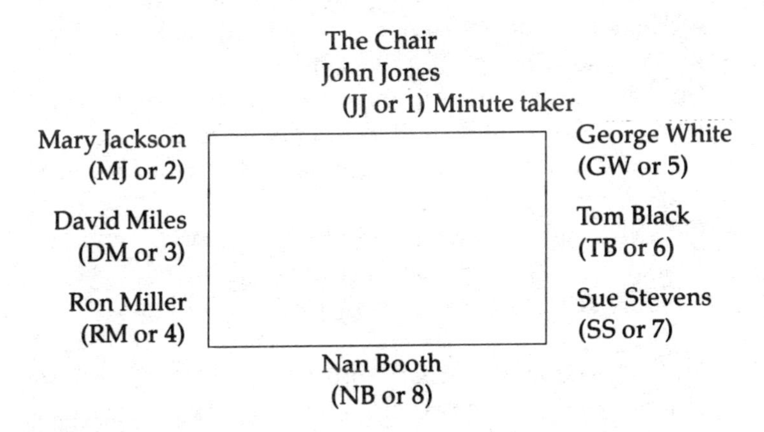

Main participants

Although this book is primarily concerned with the work of the minute taker, the other participants affect the efficiency or lack of it in the proceedings. Their role can therefore impinge on the quality of the minutes.

The most important person is the meeting leader. He or she

may be called Mr or Madam Chairman or similar names, and be referred to as the Chair or Chairperson, titles which might have developed from the days when furniture was costly and only a leader was permitted the luxury of a chair. If there is nothing in the rules or previous minutes to guide you, and it is the first time you are taking the minutes, ask the 'leader' as soon as possible before the meeting begins what he or she prefers to be called. As minute taker you know the qualities required to do your job well. You would probably also like to know (and will soon discover) what makes a good Chair. The following is a guideline in case you are ever asked to deputise in his or her absence. A good Chair:

- Starts the meeting on time, introduces and welcomes all newcomers.
- Knows the meeting's objectives.
- Ensures that the agenda (about which more will be said later) is prepared and circulated before the meeting and that necessary material and staff resources are available. These tasks are sometimes allocated to the secretary or minute taker.
- Knows the rules and follows them.
- Makes a clear statement of the issues to be discussed.
- Sees that facts are stated accurately and fully.
- Assigns the floor to whoever wishes to speak, but sees that no one monopolises it.
- Restricts tactless remarks and the discussion of opinions or experiences when facts are available.
- Ensures that each side of an issue is fully and fairly stated.
- Makes frequent verbal summaries of conclusions reached and restates all motions, amendments and the result of any voting, casting the deciding vote in the case of a tie.
- Names the proposers and seconders of motions if these names are to appear in the minutes.
- Ends the meeting on time, sets the time and date for a future meeting.

Other participants

Other participants in the meeting, though not so important as the Chair, may or may not contribute to the effectiveness of the meeting, for some come not to achieve the meeting's objectives but for aims of their own. Some of these hidden aims are revealed in Chapter 4, which deals with the agenda. Chapter 6 discusses different formats for the writing of minutes, depending on company policy and its house style.

CHAPTER 4
The Agenda

Contents

What goes into the agenda? This is an easy question to answer as many of the items come up in one form or another at every meeting. Standard headings can cover these matters, and as their appearance is so frequent they should be numbered, abbreviated and set out in a logical order.

A typical agenda from an editorial advisory board meeting is illustrated below. The agenda starts, as usual, with the following:

- Apologies for absence.
- Minutes of the previous (or last) meeting come next. They should have been circulated beforehand so that they do not now have to be read.
- Matters arising from the minutes usually follows this item.

The full text appears as follows:

Editorial Advisory Board Meeting

On . . . Time . . . Date . . . Place . . .

AGENDA

1. Apologies for absence
2. Minutes of the meeting held on (*time*)
3. Matters arising

4. Review of recent issue
5. Update on existing forthcoming features
6. Recent industry developments
7. Suggestions for new forthcoming features
8. European developments
9. Any other business
10. Date of next meeting

The purpose of the item 'Matters arising' is to inform committee members of developments that have arisen since the business of the last meeting and for which no provision has been made on any other part of the agenda.

Sequence

It can be seen that matters arising, normally placed third on the agenda, could mean a retracing of steps, going over what has already been discussed before. Such a sequence at the beginning of the meeting may cause some members to feel that they are wasting their time. Another disadvantage of matters arising having an early place is that it often becomes difficult to separate discussion of future actions from those already taken. Lastly, matters arising can provide the opportunity for somebody to reopen a discussion on decisions already made, and so waste yet more time. In these circumstances a strong Chair is needed.

A more orderly progression can be achieved when the minute taker arranges the agenda with the Chair. If this is not possible, go through the minutes of the previous meeting. Separate the subjects which need a report or continued discussion. List them in another part of the agenda, perhaps as or contained within 'any other business' (AOB), and before the last item which should be the date of the next meeting.

An example of the first three items on an average agenda sheet is given overleaf:

Meeting of Hawthorn Committee to be held on Thursday 18 February 199X at 11 am at the Garden Centre SP1.

AGENDA

Welcome by Chair (*optional*) to newcomers and guests

1. Apologies for absence
2. Minutes of meeting held on . . .
3. Matters arising

Unless there are legal rules governing what is to be discussed, the above items will be followed by topics which depend on the committee's function and work. They could be reports from the treasurer or secretary, correspondence or special group business. Examples at an editorial board meeting might be 'recent industry developments' or; 'suggestions for forthcoming features'. In the health and safety committee of a factory, there might be items on parking problems, new computer systems and health regulations. Reports may also come from subcommittees formed for a special task, eg, finance subcommittee, fête subcommittee.

Whatever the nature of the topics discussed, unless there is an adjournment, the meeting always concludes with the item any other business and the date of the next meeting. It is useful to prepare a two-column agenda for the Chair. Notes or guidelines can then be written in one column, adjacent to the main agenda. The following is an example:

AGENDA	CHAIR'S AGENDA (*or notes*)
Welcome by Chair (*optional*)	Congrats to Mrs Cole (Jenny Addams) on the birth of her baby. Returning to work after maternity leave on . . .
1. Apologies for absence	Jack Johnson out of hospital hoping to return next week

2. Minutes of meeting held on . . .	Minutes
3. Matters arising	From AOB last meeting. Planning officer away at Nice conference until next month

If time is the paramount consideration as it can be in some circumstances, the two-column agenda can similarly be used, with topics for discussion given a time against them, as in the following example:

AGENDA	TIME
Editorial board meeting	3 hours (total)
Suggestions for forth-coming features	30 mins
Health regulations	15 mins
New computer systems	45 mins
Parking problems	20 mins

1. Apologies for absence

This item includes not only those who attended the meeting but also those who were sent invitations and did not come. Some meetings cannot begin without a certain number of people being present. The actual minimum number or *quorum* as it is called, which is required for the meeting to take place, will be found in the rules or standing orders of the organisation. The late arrival or early departure of members must be noted in the minutes because it changes the number of people at the meeting, and if there is not a quorum no vote can be taken. Any that is will have no validity. People who are not members of the committee but have been asked to attend the meeting, perhaps because they can contribute to its prestige or the discussions, are registered separately as 'in attendance'. The following example shows how this is reported in the minutes:

> Minutes of Hawthorn Editorial Advisory Board held at the Ballroom, NE19
>
> PRESENT
>
> **Editorial Advisory Board**
>
> John Doe
> Mary Smith
> Tom Jones
> Ann Brown
>
> **Hawthorn Publishing**
>
> John Hawthorn (Chairman)
> Bob Fuller
>
> **Apologies for Absence**
>
> Mike Toofree
>
> **In Attendance**
>
> Sir Harry Braggart

2. Minutes of previous meeting

The ways in which this item can be recorded depend on whether the minutes for the previous meeting are circulated before or read at the current meeting; and whether there was any disagreement from members about the wording in the previous minutes or an agreement to a change in the recorded minutes. If the reading of the minutes of the previous meeting was deferred or dispensed with, this fact is recorded in the current minutes.

These situations are usually recorded in the following way:

- Minutes of meeting (*date*) were approved as circulated. OR
- Minutes of meeting (*dated*) were approved as read. OR
- Minutes of the meeting held (*date*) were approved with corrections.

Corrections. The larger the meeting, the more important it is that any suggested corrections should come in advance. This gives you a chance to read the corrections and see if they change the effect of decisions. Minute changing is a common and clever form of revisionism. Be on your guard. You can accept that the minute was wrong and alter it; insist that it was correct and refuse to alter it; or negotiate with the objector(s) an acceptable form of words. The outcome can be resolved by a simple vote of the people who were present at the meeting when the disputed minutes were taken. If it is agreed that they were incorrectly recorded, the minute taker strikes through the offending portion of the minutes, writes the new version in longhand above, dates the correction and asks the chair to initial it. The record now reads thus:

Minutes of meeting held (*date*) were approved with corrections.

3. Matters arising

This item is usually about minor matters that have arisen from the previous minutes and, as has already been stated, can be postponed to a later part of the agenda.

4. Reports

Reports can be received, presented, considered or adopted. *Received* indicates that the report was sent to the committee or the committee officer for information only. When that information is conveyed or explained orally, the report is said to be *presented*. The report is *considered* when the group discusses it and takes no further action. When the report contains opinions or facts and ends with a resolution, the committee can accept that resolution or not. If the resolution is accepted or *adopted*, that result is noted in the minutes. A special word of caution is needed if the meeting asks for the resolution to be 'entered in the minutes'. The complete report must then be included in the minutes. After the report has been adopted, it might be amended, and the emendation needs also to be entered. Matters discussed under reports can be given sub-headings, thus:

Launch of newsletter by supplements editor.

4.1 JH considered this a good idea (item in report underlined).
4.2 MM moved that the art editor should prepare a dummy copy before the next committee meeting.
4.3 Motion seconded by WW.
4.4 Motion carried on a show of hands.

Finances
The finances of the group may be discussed under the treasurer's report. In voluntary societies this is usually an account of the money in hand. In larger, more formal, meetings it is more detailed, but in neither case is it approved until audited. The Chair thanks the treasurer and states that the accounts will be filed. At an annual general meeting, the treasurer's report will be presented in printed or written form and audited in line with the rules governing the organisation which votes whether to accept it.

6. Correspondence
Letters sent to the group are recorded under this section as are fax messages and telephone conversations. Again, as with reports, if the letters are lengthy they should be attached to the minutes or filed, and a note made of where they are kept.

7. Any other business
This item allows for any item not mentioned on the agenda (a last-minute development, perhaps) to be discussed. It also gives the opportunity to express thanks to those who might not have been mentioned under the Chair's agenda. This part of the proceedings may also include the assignation of particular

tasks to particular members, and any deadlines which have to be met.

8. Adjournment or close

When the meeting is adjourned or closed, the minute taker records 'The chair adjourned the meeting at (*giving the time*)', or 'There being no further business, the meeting closed at . . .', similarly giving the time when the meeting ended.

9. Next meeting

The date, time and place of the next meeting is recorded before the assembly leaves. The minute taker's signature appears at the end of the minutes.

Hidden agendas

The above list covers most of the items likely to appear on an agenda, but in addition to this explicit list there is often a hidden agenda. The meeting may have been called for one purpose, for example, to agree on a course of action, a new strategy, a merger, but the object of certain attendees is to thwart the meeting for various reasons of their own.

There are other objectives for people coming to a meeting. They may want to impress others not invited to attend or to discredit a rival, especially if the rival is not present. They may want to show superiority, perhaps by having a special report on the agenda, to work out their frustrations or problems on other members, gain promotion by turning in a performance which attracts the attention of superiors, build an empire by having people report to them, make life difficult for others, possibly by calling the meeting at an inconvenient time, defend their territory by making it seem more important, make life easier for themselves by allocating to others tasks they don't want to do, keeping tasks they would like for themselves, and continuing to discuss a topic which appears on another part of the agenda.

All sorts of reasons impel or persuade people to attend a meeting. A perspicacious minute taker will learn a lot, not only from what is said but also how it is said.

CHAPTER 5
Rules of Meetings

When people meet to start up an association, a campaign or project, or to decide on a plan of action, they try to get some sort of order in their meetings to avoid chaos. Planning, such as that for an appeals committee, may have to start months in advance of the first committee meeting. Names of those who, it is hoped, will serve on such a committee will have to be carefully researched, for they need to be personally committed to the appeal, whatever it may be, and some, at least, preferably wealthy.

Whatever its aim, a committee works better if a certain procedure or set of rules are followed. Once such rules are adopted, they help to govern the conduct of future meetings and the records made of them. It is therefore useful for minute takers to know at least some of the rules which apply to the particular meeting they are attending. Other participants, too, will know in which direction the meeting should be moving. In limited companies and public authorities many of the rules for meetings are laid down by law.

Standing orders

The first set of organisational rules (other than those of limited companies and public authorities, as mentioned above), will be drafted to suit the needs of the group. One person may be allocated this task or a smaller group, often known as a steering committee. The rules may specify who is to hold a particular office such as secretary or treasurer, the person who will take the minutes and who will be the leader (or chairperson) of the group. A maximum length of time may also be laid down for the holding of these offices by the named persons.

When agreed and finalised, the rules are presented to the parent group at an annual general meeting (AGM). Once approved, they become the accepted rules of the organisation, a code of practice often referred to as 'standing orders'.

If a participant at a meeting believes the rules are not being followed, he or she can challenge what is being said or done on a 'point of order'. Points of order usually have priority over other matters, so the leader or chairperson will have to decide whether the point is a valid one and, if so, when it should be discussed – immediately or later.

When a point of order arises, or disagreements are voiced, you may be asked, as minute taker, whether anything on the matter has been previously mentioned. It is always therefore a useful precaution to bring to the meeting, a simplified book of rules so that you can refer to them. To avoid disorder – not always easy if there are determined opponents in a meeting – the first set of rules should be written in simple language for easy understanding, in short paragraphs for easy quoting and numbered for easy reference. The meaning of any abbreviation should be given in full before its first use, and the rules may include a provision that a committee can refuse membership, without giving reasons, to any applicant. A minute taker who comes to the meeting when the rules have already been drawn up will have to take them as in place, and follow their order until they are changed.

Changing the rules

In the case of the resignation of certain officers or similar matters of importance, it becomes necessary to change the rules. The means for doing this should be in the rules themselves. Changes can take place if agreed at the AGM or by a majority of two-thirds or three-quarters of those voting on the proposal. The changes must be recorded with the date of the meeting and the authority for its change.

Motions

A formal proposal at a meeting by a member is usually introduced by the words, 'I move that . . .', and is therefore known as a motion (see page 36). The motion should be precisely worded with a clear objective so that all who hear it understand it. A member who agrees with the motion gives his or her approval by seconding it. If the motion is not seconded it has to be abandoned and does not need to be recorded in the minutes.

After the motion has been seconded, and provided there are no amendments (see below), a vote or discussion on the proposal takes place. A good Chair will restate the motion so that everyone understands it, which also helps the minute taker to note it down with the name of proposer and seconder.

Depending on the rules, the motion may be passed by a majority show of hands or by a ballot. In some meetings the figures may be recorded showing so many in favour, so many against and so many abstaining. The latter figure is useful in a big meeting as it helps to show the support (or lack of it) for the motion and also as a check on the total number of votes cast. When approved unanimously, the decision can be recorded in the minutes as 'carried nem con' (*nemine contradicente*), meaning carried without contradiction. A motion can be amended, and even an amendment can be amended – but on amendments at least, the buck stops there.

The following three examples show how a motion might appear in the minutes. The style can be altered to suit the type of committee or the minute taker's preference, provided names and subject matter are accurate:

1. Motion: it was MOVED by Penny Henry and SECONDED by Twopence Plain that the report of the cricket club should be received. Motion PASSED (or CARRIED).
2. Motion: it was MOVED by John Smith and SECONDED by Henry James that the contract for printing name-cards should be awarded to Drawrite Printers. Amending

Motion: It was MOVED by Mary Janes and SECONDED by Tom Jeans that the motion be amended to 'for a fee not exceeding £800'. The amending motion and the main motion CARRIED.

3. It was MOVED by Sarah Teesdale and SECONDED by Fiona Wyatt that £200 be set aside for new crockery in the staff canteen. Motion DEFEATED.

Three special types of motion relevant to the more formal type of meeting are discussed below. Minute takers are unlikely to come up against all of them, but knowing them can be a useful defence when a meeting is attended by people who are intent on thwarting its aims.

Privileged motions

Motions which relate to the safety, comfort and orderliness of members take precedence over all other motions. They cannot be debated and are not related to the main motion. They include the following:

- To adjourn or recess.
- To call for the orders of the day (that is the agenda or items to be discussed at that meeting).
- Questions of privilege (such as an issue which affects the honour of a member).
- To set the time of the next meeting.

Subsidiary motions

Subsidiary motions arise out of the main action. Those which cannot be debated are (1) those to limit or extend the discussion or (2) close it. Because motions (1) and (2) infringe on members' rights they usually need a two-thirds majority before they can be passed.

Incidental motions

These must be decided before main or subsidiary motions are taken and have precedence over them. They include motions to:

- appeal against a decision by the Chair;
- suspend the rules;
- object to considering the question;
- reading papers (which means reading papers before voting); and
- withdraw a motion.

Precedence of motions

The number of motions that could be raised at a meeting might be so large that they could overwhelm not only the Chair but also the minute taker, so the following list gives their order of importance and the precedence in which they are ranked:

- Fix the time of the next meeting.
- Adjourn.
- Recess (a brief interruption in a meeting).
- Questions of privilege.
- Call for the orders of the day.
- Appeal.
- Lay on the table (phrase common in trade union meetings where an issue is to remain open without a decision being made).
- To close a debate.
- To limit or extend it.
- Postpone definitely.
- Commit or refer. (These two expressions, which mean the same thing, are a motion made when an issue requires further attention or which would take up too much time to debate in the meeting itself. A special group may then be set up to discuss the matter or, if such a group already exists, the matter will be referred to it.)
- Amend.
- Postpone indefinitely.
- Main motion.

If a motion of higher-ranking precedence is raised when another motion is being discussed, then the lower one becomes out of order and the higher ranking motion must be discussed instead.

Example
John Jones moves that the product committee begin work on the packaging. If Mary Smith then moves to postpone this motion, her motion is valid because it has a higher ranking than the main one from John Jones. However, Jack Thomson then asks for a recess. This has a higher precedence still, and the meeting will be temporarily postponed; no amendment is possible this time, because a recess is higher than a postponement.

Resolutions

Just as a bill becomes an Act when it is passed by Parliament, so a motion becomes a resolution when it is passed at a conference or a formal committee meeting. It should contain no jargon or abbreviations and be clear and unambiguous. If the meeting is a very formal or high-powered one, such as a parliamentary committee or an important conference meeting, the title of the organisation moving the resolution should be given; if it is a request for action, the title of the group to whom the resolution will be forwarded should also be given. Resolutions are, in effect, motions which result in action and are not usually subject to amendments or points of order. In informal meetings they are sometimes made in the form of a suggestion which is not mandatory, and the minutes therefore record it in a similar form, such as, 'It was AGREED that . . .' Often resolutions are used to confer an award.

Example

> The Choral Society moved the adoption of the following resolution: that in consideration of the work of Steve Bench who is now retiring . . .

it is RESOLVED that a plaque should be presented to him with thanks from all the members for his services.

CARRIED nem con [that is, unanimously]

Meetings in the workplace

Formal meetings in the workplace follow all the principles outlined above except that the rules will never contain any reference to applications for membership. If you are asked by your employer(s) to attend or serve on a particular committee, you turn up – or else! The major difficulty about rules for formal meetings may be not what they are but where they are.

CHAPTER 6
Writing the Minutes: House Style

The heading of the minutes

Companies and organisations use different styles for their minutes, but one thing is nearly always constant: the beginning. For minutes (and for speeches), it is useful to remember the words of the king in Lewis Carroll's *Alice in Wonderland*, 'Begin at the beginning, . . . and go on till you come to the end; then stop.'

The beginning of the minutes is the heading. It gives the name of the company, group or organisation, and any or all of three further items: the date and the names of those present and absent. Thus:

- Hawthorn Seeds Inc

  OR
- Hawthorn Seeds Inc, Rotten Row, London E1.

When more detail is needed, for example, in which room the meeting took place, this information can be added, as in the following:

Hawthorn Seeds Inc:
Meeting of the Brassica Committee in the Glasshouse
at 2.30 pm on 1 April 199X

Sometimes an identifying number or reference for the meeting is attached:

> Hawthorn Seeds Inc:
> Meeting of the Brassica Committee in the Glasshouse
> at 2.30 pm on 1 April 199X
> Working Party Number 4

Names of those attending

After the title, date and place come the names of those attending the meeting. The Chair always heads this list. The secretary either comes next or last.

Difficulties
The list of people attending can present difficulties. Should those present have their names given in full, or by initials? Should forenames be mentioned or should participants be referred to as Mr Smith and Miss Brown rather than Mr John Smith and Miss Jane Brown?

The standard practice is to list members alphabetically and, as some people are sensitive about the use of their forenames, to use initials with their surnames. Many women, including married women, prefer the prefix Ms. Perhaps this could be ascertained before the meeting starts.

When there is a large number of participants, it does not make much sense to list perhaps 40 or more names at the beginning of the minutes, yet worse is to group them anonymously as in the following example:

Present	Mr K Fuller Chairman
	Ms M Rose Secretary and 36 other members

Far worse, however, than listing a large number of names at the beginning is to group them anonymously while giving the names of absentees in full, as in the following:

Present Mr K Fuller Chairman
Ms M Rose Secretary and 36 other members

Apologies for absence were received from Messrs J Brown, P Smith, A Thomson, C Appelbee and Mrs G Mole

One way out of this dilemma is to have members present, other than the Chair, listed in an appendix of names as suggested above, and list the apologies for absence in a horizontal line as follows:

Present Mr K Fuller Chairman
Ms M Rose Secretary
36 members present listed on Appendix A

Apologies for absence were received from Messrs J Brown, P Smith, A Thomson, C Appelbee and Mrs G Mole

Description of members

Members of the armed forces sometimes prefer to retain their military rank in civilian life, particularly if they are in positions of authority or trust such as the bursar of a college or trustee of a charity organisation. Degrees take up too much valuable space in the minutes and are rarely relevant, but honours and titles may be of importance in the context of, say, an appeals committee.

Intermittent absences

Some participants may have to leave early or wish to stay for only part of a discussion. Their arrival and departure should be entered in the minutes. You cannot, however, put Ms Brown's departure at 11.30, for example, in the same place as the list of those attending, because you do not know at the start of the meeting who, if anyone, will leave before the end. So even if during the course of your minute writing you note that Ms

Brown left at 11.30, make a note of the items for which Ms Brown was present. Thus: Ms Brown (items 3 and 4 only).

Numbering

A numbering or other system is necessary for easy references to items in the current and past minutes. You can have a sequential list such as minute 1 to minute 300 but this gets very unwieldy. An easier format is a series which starts in each year, for example 93/50, 93/51 and so on. Sub-paragraphs can be numbered (a) (b) (c) or (i) (ii) (iii) or 1:1 1:2 1:3, whichever you find easier. Whatever style you use, be consistent. Do not switch from one format to another.

Discussion

The items discussed in a meeting are taken from the agenda. If they are not discussed for any reason, a mention of this should be made in the minutes. Other items should be minuted in sequence as they occur, and given sufficient background information to make them intelligible. The minutes will also provide a (succinct) account of the discussion which took place, decisions made and any actions to be taken.

Example 1

New Product Committee (*heading*)

1. Bee Keepers' Manual (item 1 listed in agenda)

> Background
>
> **1.1** GG reported on her meeting with YZ and the KDA on 12 Dec. After initial hesitation, it appeared that the KDA would be interested in collaborating or developing a book for this market.

Discussion
1.2 It was agreed that though it would be very useful to have the KDA involved in the project, they must keep to our outline (see minutes 12/90).

Decision
1.3 GG suggested a formal proposal and subsequent contract should be made.

Action
1.4 YZ was instructed by JH to proceed with the signing of the contract before September.

Example 2

Background	Mrs Malley (Reception) said that she had not received enough prospectuses for the new term in spite of several requests for them.
Discussion	Mr Taylor (Enrolments) said he was very concerned about this as he had made several representations to the Publicity Department about the situation.
Decision	Mrs Ross (Publicity) said that the delay had been due to sickness both in the publicity and printing sections. She had sympathised with their difficulties but told them, through Mr Winkler (Communications), that unless they could produce on time the contract would be terminated.

Action	Mr Winkler (Communications) said that further prospectuses were now being printed and should be ready for delivery next week.

Some minute writers (and chairpersons) prefer action notes as follows:

Action notes

Meeting . . .

Agenda item	Action	Person responsible	Date
1.			
2.			
3.			
4.			

Sometimes minutes will be typed with a large right-hand margin, headed 'Action', and the initials of the persons responsible for taking action will be inserted by each item.

Coverage of agenda items

Although items in the agenda are minuted in sequence, a particular difficulty remains of how much space to give to each item. One way of dealing with this problem is to see how much time is taken up with discussing the item in question. Although minor matters sometimes take up far more time than they should, nevertheless more space for longer discussions is a good rule of thumb.

Attribution

Financial items, too, are significant, especially when the cost of failure is high. So too but perhaps to a lesser degree is the status or seniority of contributors. Remarks made by the director-general, general manager or chief executive must be given due weight in the minutes, which leads to a further difficulty of attribution. Should the names of contributors be given or not? The following rules may prove useful. Give the names of contributors in the following cases:

- Somebody has reservations about a topic agreed by all the rest.
- A person asks for his or her name and/or contribution to be minuted.
- Members are the representatives of particular groups such as trade unions, health and safety personnel or county or district councillors.

Language of the minutes

The ABCs of accuracy, brevity and clarity have been mentioned elsewhere, but there are certain other points of language and style to consider when writing minutes. For formal or high-powered meetings it is preferable to use full sentences. But for less formal meetings there is no reason why, provided ambiguity is avoided, abbreviations should not be used in the minutes; or indeed a personal shorthand system, provided it can be easily understood and later used for writing out the minutes in full.

An example is given overleaf.

Example

Abbreviations	Minutes as written
Features list updated to delete part backlog (MR) US compensation schemes topical (JB) Broaden subject: Sweden, EEC? (MB) Series different countries? (DW) MR will contact MB (writes *Dumbfile*)	The forthcoming features list was updated and those felt to be out of date were deleted. MR explained that there was still a backlog of articles waiting to go in. JB commented that the issue of US compensation schemes was topical. MB suggested that the subject could be broadened, perhaps to include Sweden or other European countries. DW proposed a series of articles, each dealing with a different country. MR said he would contact MB who writes the *Dumbfile* pages.

Finally, remember that minutes are not meant to be literary masterpieces. They are not intended to inspire, entertain, amuse or even to move the reader, but they should be well written, that is clear and unambiguous, grammatical and, possibly, even interesting. Although their purpose is functional, that should not prevent you from giving an accurate, factual succinct report of a meeting which took place, and which you are recording for future use and inspection.

CHAPTER 7

Checklist - Before, During and After the Meeting

Before the meeting - heading

(Name of the committee, date, time and place of the meeting, as shown on page 45.)

Check these items with the chairperson (Chair) before the meeting and ensure that they are on the heading. (See illustration page 45.) Does the agenda given you by the Chair cover points left undecided at the last meeting? If necessary, point out the need to alter agenda.

Before the meeting - distribution

Send out forward notice of meeting, together with the suggested agenda: *time, date, day, place.* Emphasise latest date for any changes in agenda. (For specimen agenda, see page 34.)

Before the meeting - attendance

- Obtain copies of previous minutes or use other means to find out the distribution list.
- Check names on the above list. Consult with Chair over any deletions or additions (staff promotions, retirements, addresses, titles etc).
- Immediately prior to the meeting, that is on arrival of delegates/members and before the Chair speaks, circulate an attendance list for signature, showing name, address

and status. This is a help for inaugural meetings and when people coming from different sections of an organisation are unknown to one another. An attendance list may also be necessary for security reasons.

Before the meeting - venue

- Check venue is available (large enough? Refreshments necessary?).
- Check that the venue has sufficient seating, writing materials, special equipment, heating/air conditioning or other facilities.

Before the meeting - carry-in material

Take with you all necessary appendices or exhibits and make sure that they are numbered.

During the meeting

- Use, if permitted, but do not rely on, a tape-recorder.
- Cross-reference matters arising to previous minutes.
- Record too much rather than too little. Ensure that you understand each speaker, and correctly paraphrase or précis their contribution.
- If you cannot hear or understand any speaker, ask them to repeat or clarify what they have said. Read their statement aloud before you note it down so that there can be no disagreement later as to its veracity.
- Record the time when the meeting starts. If the Chair has not arrived by the scheduled time, a Deputy Chair or some other officer should take over the meeting until the Chair arrives. Enter these facts in the minutes.
- Record late arrivals and early departure times in case this reduces the numbers then present at the meeting below the minimum necessary for a quorum.

- Record everything as it happens even if this is not the order listed in the agenda. Such a change may be due to the early leaving of some committee member and this may have important consequences for the rest of the meeting.
- As the Chair moves through the agenda, he or she can miss items on the agenda. Point out quickly any such lapses.
- Record the name of proposer and seconder of any formal propositions made at the meeting.
- If anybody protests in a discussion (often against a majority view) and asks for that protest to be 'minuted, please', take down what is said and read it out aloud so that it is agreed by all present to be exactly what the speaker has said.
- Ensure that any action to be taken before the next meeting is given a timescale and that there is no confusion about when it is to be done and by whom. Highlight their names and those to whom they are to report.
- The time of the meeting's closure should be noted. If some outside situation or emergency arises which brings the meeting to an end before the agenda is finalised, and the meeting is therefore adjourned, this fact must be noted in the minutes.
- When the meeting is resumed, it is a continuation of the original meeting. The names of people present, the time and place should be noted, but as this is not a new meeting the minutes should continue as Part 2. Decisions are only valid if taken at the closure of a meeting, not before a break, however caused.
- Before members disband, make sure they know the date, time and place of next meeting agreed by all present.

After the meeting

- Using your recorder and/or notes, prepare a rough draft of what happened at the meeting. Use the format of previous minutes or, if this is the first meeting of its kind, organise your own minutes unless a certain kind of layout is favoured by your company (or manager) or laid down in any rules.
- Present the rough draft to the Chair for his or her approval and/or emendation as necessary.
- Prepare a final copy of minutes, paragraph and number them. Do not use a loose-leaf pad or shorthand notebook, even if this has previously been the custom. It is not unknown for a vital page to go missing . . . accidentally. Get Chair's approval to forward a copy of the minutes to each person present at the meeting, together with other distribution channels suggested by the Chair.

Glossary

Ab initio A Latin phrase meaning 'from the beginning'. (Latin phrases can be useful abbreviations for the English equivalents.)

Abstain Deliberately to refrain from voting.

Addendum Which adds words.

Addressing the Chair By convention a committee member speaks as if only to the Chair.

Ad hoc For this occasion. An *ad hoc* committee is one set up for a particular purpose and then abandoned.

Adjourn To stop the meeting and meet again at a later date and/or at another place.

Agenda A list of the items which a committee is to consider.

Amend To change an item by adding, inserting or removing a word or words from a motion.

Call to order A call by the chair for members to return to the business in hand and (possibly) cease unruly behaviour. Invoked when a meeting is ready to start formally.

Casting vote Vote cast by the Chair in favour of one side or the other when the vote has been equal; it decides the winner.

Censure An official reprimand.

Composite motion A motion which combines several motions on the same subject.

Constitution The rules governing the objectives, structure and functions of an organisation.

Convene Call a meeting.

Declaration of interest Declaration by a member of the meeting that he or she has an interest in the subject to be discussed; usually a financial interest is involved.

De facto Actually existing though not because of a legal right to do so.

De jure By right, though this does not mean something actually exists.

Delegate A person chosen to represent others at a meeting or conference.

Ex officio member A member by reason of the office held who cannot vote but must receive all the reports, agendas and minutes.

Fiscal year The financial year of an organisation.

Guillotine Cutting of discussion of a topic at a fixed time fixed in advance.

Mandate An authoritative instruction or command.

Modus operandi A method of working.

Motion (main) A proposal put before a meeting to be discussed before a decision is made. When passed it becomes a resolution.

Nem con (Nemine contradicente) Unanimous agreement with nobody dissenting.

Out of order Not in accordance with the rules.

Point of information Information passed via the Chair to a person during the course of his or her speech.

Point of order Question to the Chair requiring an answer, which interrupts the business of the meeting.

(To) postpone indefinitely (or *sine die*) To adjourn a motion when an item requires further investigation or the discussion might be too time consuming. The issue may then be referred to a special group. This motion sometimes effectively kills off any debate of the item until some uncertain future date.

Proposer of a motion The first person to speak on a motion.

Pro tem For the time being.

Proxy Someone who votes for another, with their agreement.

Quorum The minimum number of people who must be present for a meeting to take place.

Refer back or remit To forward a proposal for a committee to decide.

Rescind To cancel a previous action.

Resolution Motion which has been approved.

Seconder The first person to support (or second) a motion.

Standing orders The rules which govern the conduct of a meeting.

Sub judice Under consideration.

Suspend the rules To change the order of the agenda; requires a two-thirds vote.

Teller A person appointed to count votes.

Terms of reference The boundaries within which an item is discussed.

Ultra vires Beyond a body's legal powers.

Verbatim Word for word.

Veto The power of a person or body to prevent a proposal being acted upon.

Appendix
Formal Minutes

It should not be thought that, because minutes are formally presented, they are therefore perfect examples of good minute writing. Whether they are good or bad, however, much can be learnt from them: the use of many alternatives (regrets, deplores, notes, believes, etc as in the example) to the word 'said'; how minutes are amended; the use of appendices to supply further information; the numbering of pages, motions and minutes. There are negative lessons, too, in the art of précis that you can learn by studying the formal minutes of some committee meetings, even if, owing to the composition of its members, those lessons can only be put into practice elsewhere.

You can obtain a copy of formal minutes such as those of a council meeting from the council offices or borrow them from the local library. The following is an example of the minutes of a council meeting of the London Borough of Sutton.

In the original format, the minutes extended over 24 pages of small print, and the meeting itself lasted from 7 pm until 11.50 pm. Readers looking at a copy of minutes of such length in a book of this kind might find their eyes glazing over. To save them from this fate, the minutes have therefore been summarised with enough headings and examples to show procedures and the general thrust of the discussions. It is interesting to note that in several sections, the present tense is used. (The

Council believes that, etc), but not for motions, resolutions, amendments, or questions under standing orders. The page numbers (footers) of the printed minutes are given in the example opposite and follow the last sentence on any given page of the minutes.

Extracts from the minutes are reproduced by kind permission of the London Borough of Sutton.

Example of formal minutes

Council, 8 March 1993

London Borough of Sutton

MINUTES

of the meeting of the Council
of the London Borough of Sutton held
in the Europa Gallery, Civic Offices,
Sutton on Monday 8 March 1993 at 7 pm

MEMBERS

The Worshipful the Mayor
(Councillor Joan Dutton MCSP)

The Deputy Manager
(Councillor Frank Sharp C Eng FIEE)

Councillors

(Here follows some 54 names with their academic and other qualifications. Asterisks are marked against 5 names. At the bottom of the 3 column list, the asterisk is shown to indicate absences: (*Absent))

690. MINUTES

Resolved: That the minutes of the meeting of the Council held on 11 January 1993 having been circulated, be taken as read and signed by the Mayor.

691. MR PETER HIRST, BOROUGH ARCHITECT AND PLANNING OFFICER

Here the Mayor refers to Minute 608 and the impending retirement of the above officer. Named members associate themselves and their parties with the sentiments expressed in that Minute.

692. QUESTIONS

In accordance with Notice given under Standing Order 7 (ii), questions and supplementary questions were asked and replies given thereto as set out in Appendix A to these Minutes.

693. PETITIONS

(i) (Here a Councillor presents a petition opposing the transfer of a local hospital) which, in accordance with Standing Order 4 (i) (i) stood referred to the Policy and Resources Committee.

(ii) The Chief Executive reported the receipt of a petition under Standing Order 13A organised by protesting at . . . In accordance with Standing Order 13A, the petition stood referred to the Housing and Social Services Committee.

End of page **427**

(iii) (Another) petition stood referred to the Highways and Transportation Sub-Committee.

694. NOTICES OF MOTION

(a) Anti-Poverty Strategy

In accordance with Notice given, Councillor Charlie Mansell moved:

This Council believes that . . . meet.

The Council therefore agrees to . . . and adopts the following statement of principles to be followed:

(i) This Council recognises that there is a substantial number of areas where it or indeed any local authority will have little or no impact directly on the causes and effects of poverty and that the eradication of poverty and need can only be achieved by:

(Here follows a list of principles.)
. . . the Council will use what influence it has to work for those ends.

(ii) Nonetheless an important contribution can be made. As far as the Council's own direct functions are concerned the Council is committed to:

(a) ensuring, as far as possible, that an individual's level of income does not affect their ability to participate in decisions about issues which affect them; (etc).

End of page **428**

(iii) All departments of the Council will be examining their services against these principles and in four aspects proposing action to:

(a) make services at least equally accessible to people experiencing poverty, but adopting positive action to target services towards low income groups where appropriate; (etc).

The motion was seconded by Councillor John Weir and, in accordance with Standing Order 5, was referred to the Policy and Resources Committee for consideration and report.

(b) Bus De-regulation

In accordance with Notice given Councillor John Weir moved:

(i) 'This Council notes with alarm:

(a) The appalling state of transport in the capital and the substantial traffic congestion encouraged by the lack of safe and affordable public transport; (etc).

(ii) The Council notes that:

(a) de-regulation of bus services outside London has resulted in higher fares; over-bussing and congestion on popular routes; cuts in services on quiet routes and outside peak times; and lower levels of bus use; . . .

End of page **429**

(iii) The Council rejects the Government claim that competition will give a better and cheaper service . . . The administrative costs if the London Boroughs have to negotiate with a number of bus contractors will be prohibitive.

(iv) The Council recognises the importance to pensioners and the disabled of concessionary travel permits – a universal benefit to them all. . . .

(v) Therefore this Council resolves to communicate its opposition to the above proposals to all interested parties and support all other London local authorities and local authority associations against bus de-regulation.'

The motion was seconded by Councillor Don Hopkins and, in

accordance with Standing Order 5, was referred to the Environment Services Committee for consideration and report.

695. REPORTS OF COMMITTEES

Resolved: That Part 'A' of the Minutes of the meetings of the undermentioned Committees be received and the recommendations contained therein be adopted as varied by any amendments which were carried or alterations made by the mover, as set out below:

Committee	Moved by	Date of Meeting 1993
Education	Dealt with in accordance with Minute 697 on page 436	21 January
Policy and Resources	Councillor Graham Tope (Minute 598 only) Minutes 599–609 were dealt with in accordance with Minute 697 on Page 437	18 February

In accordance with the referred priority of the political groups on the Council, consideration of Part 'A' of the Minutes of the Committee was given in the following order:

(a) **Policy and Resources Committee 18 February 1993**
Minute 598 – Revised Revenue Estimates 1992/93 and Draft Revenue Estimates 1993/4

Questions asked under Standing Order 7(i)

In accordance with Standing Order 7(i), questions and supplementary questions were asked and replies given thereto as set out in Appendix B to these Minutes.

The following attention to the Minute was made by the Chairman on reception of the Minute:

Add new recommendation:

'(iv) That the 993/1994 estimate for GLC Deemed Debt included under Special Provisions and Credits on line 11 of page 315 of Revenue Estimates 1993/1994 be reduced from £1 million to £401,000 and estimated Council balance at 31 March 1994 be increased to £2,920,300 (as shown on the attached revised page (xiv) of Revenue Estimates 1993/1994);'

Renumber remaining recommendations and substitute as follows in former recommendations (v): . . .

The Council agreed that one speaker from each of the political groups on the Council should be permitted to exceed the time limit for speeches imposed by Standing Order 9(vi) on this Minute.

End of page **430**

Councillor Rob Irving, Chairman of the Resources Sub-Committee, made a statement on the recommended Council Tax levels for 1993/1994.

An amendment was moved by Councillor Graham Tope and seconded by Councillor Steve Penneck:

Add new recommendation '(viii) This Council:

1. Welcomes the demise of the Poll Tax . . . Borough.
2. Believes that . . . Council Chamber.
3. Regrets the absence of a full public debate . . . IT'S CONFUSING.
4. Notes that . . . ability to pay.
5. Notes that single people only get a 25% discount . . . Poll Tax!
6. Believes that the Government's relief scheme is unfair . . .
7. Regrets that reductions for the disabled . . .
8. Deplores the fact that . . . improving local services.
9. Believes that . . . essential services.
10. Believes that . . . local income tax as proposed by the Liberal Democrats.'

On being put to the vote the amendment was declared carried on a show of hands.

10.14 pm The Mayor vacated the chair in favour of the Deputy Mayor.

An amendment was moved by Councillor Barber and seconded by Councillor Mrs Peart:

Delete recommendations (i) (ii) (iii) (iv) and (vi) on the basis that the original recommendation (iv) to the Minute has been renumbered (v) following the decision on GLC deemed debt.

End of page **431**

Insert

1. That recommendations (i) (ii) (iii) (iv) and (v) be amended to reflect the additional savings . . . and the adjustment to balances set out in recommendations 8 and 9 below.
2. Regrets that the Liberal Democrats are unable to fix the Budget . . . bogus consultations.
3. Notes particularly their absurd pretence that . . . political purposes.
4. This amendment shows how many of the cuts . . . over the 'cuts'.
5. (a) Welcomes the Conservative Government's efforts . . . last year's figure.
   (b) Draws the attention of Council members to the fact that the Conservative Government provides 78% of the Council's budget . . . as they wish.
   (c) Notes that Sutton now has a Standard Spending Assessment (S.S.A.) higher than that of Kingston upon Thames . . . spend on local services.
   If this claim is true why are any 'cuts' being proposed at all?
   (d) Notes that . . . fair and consistent.
6. Recalls that the majority party has claimed that Sutton's Standard Spending Assessment is calculated unfairly in relation to 'Ethnicity' and 'Unemployment'.
   (a) Ethnicity:
   notes the complaint is based on the fact that . . . against Liberal Democrat Councils.

End of page **432**

   (b) Unemployment:
   notes the Liberal Democrat campaign . . . socialist led Spain and the Republic of Ireland.
7. Reminds the majority party that . . . Members of Parliament.

8. That the following savings be incorporated in the Revenue estimates 1993/1994

		£	£
1.	Reduction in General Contingency Provision (para 6.10)	200,000	200,000
	Policy and Resources		
2.	Accelerate Contracting out of Council Services	75,000	
3.	Expedite closure of Sutton Court House	40,000	
4.	Reduction in Printing Budget	200,000	
5.	Reduction in Policy Development Unit	75,000	
6.	Centre for Environmental Information	29,300	
7.	Sutton Racial Equality Council	38,200	
8.	Sutton Women's Centre	20,500	
9.	Refugee Network Sutton	500	
10.	Repairs and Renewals	500,000	
11.	Section 11 Funding – Translators and Interpreters	7,500	
12.	Complaints Procedure – Training and Information	6,000	992,000
	Leisure Services		
13.	Mothball the Charles Cryer Theatre (p29 Budget Consultative Report)	106,600	106,600
	Total Savings		£1,298,600

9. That the following increases be incorporated in the Revenue Estimates 1993/94:

	Housing and Social Services		
1.	Increase for Care in the Community to include home carers	300,000	300,000

Education

2.	Discretionary Awards (restore)	203,000	
3.	Primary Education Aggregated Schools Budget (restore) 130,000		
4.	Secondary Education Aggregated Schools Budget (restore) 214,000		
5.	Extra Learning Support Team (restore)	50,000	
6.	Reinstate Sutton Primary Diagnostic Unit	50,000	
7.	Establish a Unit for Teenagers with behavioural difficulties 50,000		
8.	Restore Cuts to Orchard Hill Further Education Centre 20,000		
9.	Increase School Transport Budget	97,000	
10.	Restore cut to SCOLA	153,000	
11.	Youth Bands and Orchestra	10,000	
12.	Supervised Play Service	12,000	
13.	Advisory Teachers	71,300	
14.	Youth Service	50,000	
15.	Classroom Assistants for Special Schools	50,000	1,160,300

End of page **433**

Environmental Services

16.	Review of Parking Restrictions and Yellow Lines	50,000	
17.	Restore Cuts in Skip Collection and Scour Clean	200,000	
18.	Reopen Public Conveniences	50,000	300,000

Policy and Resources

19.	Installation of Video Cameras in Sutton High Street (Business to match £1 for £1)	50,000	
20.	Additional Funding for Security Force	100,000	
21.	Re-establish post of Assistant Chief Executive (Borough Solicitor)	48,000	198,000

Total Increased Expenditure	1,958,300

SUMMARY

Increased Expenditure	£1,958,300
Deduct	
Additional Savings	£1,298,600
Adjustment to Balances	£659,700

An exemplification of the amendment was circulated and is set out in Appendix C to these Minutes.

On being put to the vote the amendment was declared lost on a show of hands.

11.20 pm The Mayor resumed the chair.

An amendment was moved by Councillor John Weir and seconded by Councillor Mike Woolley:

Delete all after 'That' in (i)

Insert

'this Council condemns . . . cuts in its services.

(ii) The Council notes that . . .

(iii) In view of the severity of the cuts and the need to protect essential services this Council agrees to the expenditure and Collection Fund levels set out in the attached annex to this recommendation.

(iv) This recommendation reverses all cuts in Education and Social Services, which we consider priority areas of Council service.

(v) As a result of (iii) and (iv) above, this Council reluctantly must join . . .

(vi) This Council believes that the Secretary of State must be blamed if he insists on Sutton staying with expenditure limits and that he will be responsible for the cuts in Education and Social Services.'

An exemplification of the amendment was circulated and is set out in Appendix D to these Minutes.

On being put to the vote the amendment was declared lost on a show of hands.

The Minute, as altered and amended, was adopted in the following terms:

696. Resolved (i) That the recommendations in Minute 655/93 (Revised Revenue Estimates 1992/93 and draft Revenue Estimates 1993/94) including the decisions of the Housing and Social Services and Education Committees in Minutes 407/93 and 454/93 be adopted;

End of page **434**

(ii) That the precepts and levies from other authorities and organisations be noted and taken into account;

(iii) That the budget required for 1993/94 for grant maintained schools be amended to £14,175,000;

(iv) That the 1993/94 estimate for GLC Deemed Debt (included under Special Provisions and Credits on line 11 of Page 315 of Revenue Estimates 1993/94) be reduced from £1 million to £401,000 and estimated Council balances at 31 March 1994 be increased to £2,920,300 (as shown on attached revised page (xiv) of Revenue Estimates 1993/94 – Appendix E to these Minutes);

(v) That it be noted that at the meeting of 11 January 1993 the Council calculated the amount of £66,900 as its Council Tax Base for the year 1993/94 in accordance with Regulation 3 of the Local Authorities (Calculation of Council Tax Base) Regulations 1992 made under Section 33(5) of the Local Government Finance Act 1992;

(vi) That the following amounts be now calculated by the Council for the year 1993/94 in accordance with Sections 32 to 36 of the Local Government Finance Act 1992: . . .

End of page **435**

(vii) That sincere thanks be conveyed to the Director of Finance and his staff for their efforts in producing the revenue estimates 1993/94 and to all Directors and their staff for ensuring that this year's estimates were on target.

(viii) This Council:

1. Welcomes the demise of the Poll Tax . . .
2. Believes that the Poll Tax was an ill-conceived tax . . .
3. Regrets the absence of a full public debate . . .
4. Notes that the Government's Council Tax is a tax on property and bears no relation to ability to pay . . .
5. Notes that single people only get a 25% discount so most will pay more than they did under the Poll Tax . . .
6. Believes that the Government's relief scheme is unfair . . .
7. Regrets that reductions for the disabled do not apply to those in band A . . .
8. Deplores the fact that the Government's Council Tax has already cost the country £250 million to value properties into bands . . .
9. Believes that the Government's 'capping' regulations are even harsher than under the Poll Tax . . .
10. Believes that the Government's Council Tax is no better than the Poll Tax it replaces.

697. STANDING ORDER 9(XX)

On the motion of Councillor Graham Tope, seconded by Councillor Steve Penneck, it was:

Resolved: That all motions remaining to be dealt with at the meeting for the reception and consideration of Part 'A' of the Reports and Committees (including the alteration to Minute 603 as set out below) be received and adopted.

The Minutes affected by this decision and thereby adopted were as follows:

(a) Education Committee – 21 January 1993
Minute 398 – Petition – Sutton Primary Diagnostic Unit
Dissent was expressed by the Conservative Group
The Labour Group expressed dissent as the Group wished to retain the Sutton Primary Diagnostic Unit, albeit in alternative premises
Minute 399 – Establishment of a Consortium for the Registered Inspection of Schools

(b) Policy and Resources Committee – 18 February 1993
Minute 599 – Motion: Queen Mary's Hospital

Minute 600 – Standing Orders
Minute 601 – Guidance for Councillors on Accepting Gifts and Hospitality
Minute 602 – Duties, Functions and Powers of the Council, Committees and Sub-Committees
Minute 603 – Appointment of Representatives on other Bodies: Appeals Committee Panel – Education Act 1981 – Sections 7 and 8
The Minute was adopted subject to the addition of Councillor Sue Stears to the membership.
Minute 604 – London Local Authorities (2) Bill 1993
Minute 605 – CCT Implications for the Employment Bill and Transfer of Undertakings (Employment Protection) Regulations 1981
Dissent was expressed by the Labour Group
Minute 606(640) – Policy Sub-Committee: Strategic Initiatives
Dissent was expressed by the Conservative Group
Dissent was expressed by the Labour Group
Minute 606(646) – Policy Sub-Committee: Section 11 Funding
Dissent was expressed by the Conservative Group
Minute 606(653) – Policy Sub-Committee: The Possible Merger of the Merton and Sutton Health Authority with the Wandsworth Health Authority
Dissent was expressed by the Conservative Group
Dissent was expressed by the Labour Group
Minute 607 – Resources Sub-Committee
Minute 608 – Peter Hirst, Borough Architect and Planning Officer
Minute 609 – Hazardous Waste Collection Service

The meeting ended at 11.50 pm.

End of page **437**

QUESTIONS: STANDING ORDER 7 (ii)

1. **Asked by Councillor Keith Martin of the Chairman of the Education Committee**
   In the context of . . .
   (a) . . .
   (b) . . .
   (c) . . .

   Reply by Councillor John Brennan, Chairman of the Education Committee
   (a) . . .
   (b) . . .
   (c) . . .

   Supplementary Question by Councillor Keith Martin
   I ask you how . . .

   Reply by Councillor John Brennan, Chairman of the Education Committee
   The whole crux of this problem is not my conscience but the rush to gain grant maintained status . . .

2. **Asked by Councillor Mrs Peart of the Chairman of the Education Committee**
   When did he write . . . and what reasons did he give?

End of page **438**

   Reply by Councillor John Brennan, Chairman of the Education Committee
   It was not possible to inform . . .

   Supplementary Question by Councillor Mrs Peart
   Could he explain to . . .

   Reply by Councillor John Brennan, Chairman of the Education Committee
   Mrs Peart will be well aware that . . .

3. **Asked by Councillor Barber of the Chairman of the Education Committee**
   How many secondary schools . . .

Reply by Councillor John Brennan, Chairman of the Education Committee
Five secondary schools have 'opted out' . . .

Supplementary Question by Councillor Barber
Does he now accept that . . .

Reply by Councillor John Brennan, Chairman of the Education Committee
Not really. We have had this debate on many many occasions . . .

(*and so on*).

End of page **439**

QUESTIONS: STANDING ORDER 7(i)
MINUTE 598: REVISED REVENUE ESTIMATES 1992/93
AND DRAFT REVENUE ESTIMATES 1993/94

1. **Asked by Councillor Keith Martin of the Chairman of the Policy and Resources Committee**
   Will the Chairman please advise . . .

   Reply by Councillor Graham Tope, Chairman of the Policy and Resources Committee
   This is a hypothetical question . . .

   Supplementary Question by Councillor Keith Martin
   Supposing there had been no capping limit . . .

   Reply by Councillor Graham Tope, Chairman of the Policy and Resources Committee
   It is a hypothetical question . . .

2. **Asked by Councillor Charlie Mansell of the Chairman of the Policy and Resources Committee**
   (i) Has he read the . . .
   (ii) Since the London Boroughs Association is Tory controlled would he agree with me that . . .

   Reply by Councillor Graham Tope, Chairman of the Policy and Resources Committee
   (i) Yes.
   (ii) Yes . . .

(*and so on*).

Three pages of Budget figures follow, of which only the last is reproduced.

Ref	Detail	1993/94		FORECAST	
		Estimate	Council Tax Equiv	At 1993/94 Prices	
(1)	(2)	(3)	(4)	1994/95 (5)	1995/96 (6)
		£	£	£	£
	LONDON BOROUGH OF SUTTON SERVICES				
1	Education	59,822,500	894.21	60,095,000	60,095,000
2	Environmental Services	14,703,400	219.78	14,308,000	14,511,000
3	Housing & Social Services	23,031,100	344.26	23,070,000	23,070,000
4	Leisure Services	8,422,100	125.89	8,430,000	8,430,000
5	Policy & Resources	5,808,500	86.83	7,455,000	7,455,000
6		111,787,600	1,670.97	113,358,000	113,561,000
7	Add Contingency Provision	898,000	13.42	1,581,000	2,081,000
8		112,685,600	1,684.39	114,939,000	115,642,000
	LEVIES & PRECEPTS				
9	Lee Valley Regional Park Authority	161,100	2.41	161,000	161,000
10	London Pensions Fund Authority	208,500	3.12	209,000	209,000
11	London Waste Regulation Authority	125,300	1.87	125,000	125,000
12	Merton & Sutton Joint Cemetery Board	39,700	0.59	40,000	40,000
13	National Rivers Authority	622,000	9.30	622,000	622,000
14		113,842,200	1,701.68	116,096,000	116,799,000
15	Adjustment of Balances	150,300	2.24		
16	GROSS SUTTON REQUIREMENTS RECEIPTS	113,992,500	1,703.92	116,096,000	116,799,000

17	Revenue Support Grant	(52,674,000)	(787.35)	
18	Payments from NNDR Pool	(36,235,000)	(541.63)	
19	NET SUTTON REQUIREMENTS	25,083,500	374.94	
	MEMO-BALANCES			
20	Brought Forward	2,770,000		
21	Adjustment	150,300		
22	Carried Forward	2,920,300		

COLLECTION FUND AND COUNCIL TAX

Ref	Detail	1993/94		
		Estimate	Council Tax Equiv	
(1)	(2)	(3)	(4)	
		£	£	
	PRECEPTS AND DEMANDS			
23	London Borough of Sutton	25,083,500	374.94	
24	London Fire & Civil Defence Authority	1,180,800	17.65	
25	Metropolitan Police	8,573,200	128.15	
26	TOTAL REQUIREMENTS	34,837,500	520.74	
27	Tax Base (Band D Equivalents)	66,900		

Informal Minutes

The following is an example of minutes taken at a Residents' Association meeting. It is not quite typical of many small groups that need to record what took place at meetings, for it kept strictly to the Agenda distributed earlier to members. The minutes were clearly and concisely written, and covered intelligently all the points raised, including the election of new officers. The business was completed in 90 minutes, and allowed time for refreshments after the meeting.

Example of informal minutes

The Hill Residents' Association

MINUTES of the Annual General Meeting of the The Hill Residents' Association held on 5th May 1993.

Present:

1. **Apologies for Absence**
   Cllr J Bird, Cllr Mrs O Pearl, Mrs Zebin, the Misses Gates.

2. **Minutes of the Last Meeting**
   The Minutes of the last Annual General Meeting were read by the Chairman and accepted unanimously as a true record.

3. **Treasurer's Report**
   The Accounts of the Residents' Association, copies of which had been distributed to all present, were in very good order and had been thoroughly audited by Mr J Wright.

Receipts fell slightly due to the loss of some households either through moving from the area or not renewing their membership. The other decrease was due to the change in the interest rate in the Building Society Account. The Committee will make further efforts towards increasing the number of members.

Expenditure has remained fairly constant. Assets have always been sufficient in case the regular newsletter would need to be printed commercially. So far this has not been necessary as the newsletter has been prepared and printed by members of the Committee. It has further been felt sensible to retain certain assets in the eventuality that professional help may be required at any time. However, taking all this into consideration it has not been considered necessary to increase the subscription to the Association for the time being.

Mr Biffen proposed that the Accounts be accepted which was seconded by Mr Carter. The Treasurer expressed his thanks to Mr Wright, the Auditor, for his assistance.

4. Election of Officers

The Chairman introduced the Officers and Members of the Committee some of whom would be standing down this year.

The Vice-Chairperson, Mrs Carter, offered her services for another year and this was proposed by Mr T West and seconded by Mrs Biffen.

The Treasurer, Mr David Tiles, agreed to stand for another year and this was proposed by Mrs Mayes and seconded by Mr Biffen.

It was proposed by Mrs Stanley that the Auditor, Mr Wright, be re-elected, which was seconded by Mr Tiles.

The Secretary, Mrs Mabel Wall, would be standing down this year, but no replacement was found at the meeting.

Mr John Biffen proposed that the Chairman continue for another year which was seconded unanimously.

Mrs D Tiles and Mr Charlie Hartley were both standing down from the Committee and the Chairman invited nominations from the floor.

Two nominations were received: Mrs Hartley, proposed by Mr

Biffen and seconded by Mrs Carter, and Mrs Mayes, proposed by Mrs Tiles and seconded by Mr Hartley.

The Chairman then thanked all those retiring from the Committee for their valued work during their time of office.

Index

Further Reading from Kogan Page

Effective Meeting Skills, Marion E Haynes
How to Make Meetings Work, Malcolm Peel
A Practical Guide to Effective Listening, Diane Bone
The Secretary's Survival Manual, Sandra Tomkins
Speak with Confidence, Meribeth Bunch